Orchid Care:
For The Beginner

Barb Schmidt

2015

The cover art consists of photographs I took of my own orchids. The following species are included on the cover:

- Phal Baldans Kaleidoscope
- Dtps Lioulin Orange
- Zns Murasskiko machi 'Cool Room'
- Blc Prada Green Deluxe 'NN'
- Den Children of Amaron
- Iwan Appleblossom
- Lc Angel Heart Himimanu
- L Tenebrosa
- Slc Jewel Box Scheherazade
- Phal Surf Song

To Greg, Tom and Jen

For all those years you put up with my dozens of orchid
plants around our home.

Table of Contents

Introduction

I had always admired orchids from afar. Like most people, I assumed orchid plants were the delicate, prima donnas of the plant world. Orchids were mysterious plants with exotic blooms that looked like moths or spiders and had strange names like Phalaenopsis and Paphiopedilum. I was awed by their fragile beauty and convinced that buying one would sentence it to certain death. Finally, about twelve years ago, I was entranced by the beautiful displays of flowers around me at the Philadelphia International Flower Show and decided to take the plunge. I bought my first orchid plant.

It took me several frustrating years of trial and error to figure out that raising orchids is really not rocket science. Despite any preconceptions you may have, orchids are actually fairly easy to grow once you figure out what they like. Orchid care is not difficult, it's just different from the usual house plant care. It took me almost two years to figure this out.

During those years, I tried researching orchid care and couldn't find anything that addressed the questions that a neophyte orchid enthusiast would have in terms that made sense. I needed basic, simple information that told me how to make my orchid happy in its new home. I talked to growers and attended orchid classes until I found what worked. Since then, I have had several friends visit my home and ask me for help starting their own orchid collections. I have also been asked to teach orchid classes for the Pennsylvania

Horticultural Society and two local colleges. That is what prompted me to write this book.

I should emphasize that this book is intended for the *beginner* orchid collector. It summarizes what I have learned about raising orchids. I have found that caring for orchids is mostly common sense. Once you know what these plants like when they are growing in the wild, you just have to try to replicate that in your home as best you can. That's why, throughout this book, I'll talk about the native conditions for each orchid genus. Also, orchid collecting should be fun, not a chore. I try to present simple, easy ways to raise healthy orchids that bloom consistently.

I now have over two dozen orchids in my home and ten different genera. I usually have five to ten orchids blooming at any one time. Five years ago, I came full circle and entered one of my orchids in the Philadelphia Flower Show Novice Orchid Class. I won a first place ribbon. A year later, the same orchid received an Honorable Mention in the Phalaenopsis Orchid Class. I have entered several orchids since then and won additional ribbons. It is at this point that I should mention that orchid collecting is contagious. My daughter started her own orchid collection and entered two of her own in the Novice Class. They won first and second place.

The purpose of this book is to make orchids accessible to anyone. If you follow the orchid care instructions in this book, you should be able to not only keep an orchid plant alive, but get it to bloom over and over again. I intentionally kept this book short enough to be read from cover to cover; and, I would recommend doing so as I mention various orchid care tips throughout the book. However, *Orchid Care: For the*

Beginner can also be used as a reference tool. There are chapters on specific areas of orchid care and tables at the end of the book that summarize information presented in the chapters. I also include a glossary of some of the more common orchid terms that you may not be familiar with.

The key to being successful at raising orchids is to mimic their natural conditions as best as possible without driving yourself crazy. If you meet their basic needs, most of the common household genera will adapt.

Orchidaceae –
The Orchid Family

All orchids belong to the Orchid Family, Orchidaceae. There are 880 genera and approaching 30,000 identified species of orchids in this family. New species are being identified all the time; and some botanists estimate that there may actually be as many as 50,000 different species out there. That is why orchid collecting becomes addicting — so many choices, so little time.

Proving my point that orchids are not the delicate flowers we assume they are, the orchid family has been around since the dinosaurs. Genetic sequencing shows that orchids may have arisen in the Late Cretaceous, around 76 to 84 million years ago. Orchidaceae holds the title of being one of the two largest families of flowering plants, with Asteraceae (daisies, asters and sunflowers) being the other. Orchidaceae is also considered to be the most evolved plant family, having each of its species adapted to its specific pollinator.

Orchid genera span the globe. While the majority of orchids grow naturally in tropical areas (approximately 760 genera), some genera are found above the Arctic Circle and on islands in the southwest Pacific between Australia and Antarctica. North America is home to 20 to 26 native genera; and temperate Asia and Europe have 40 to 60 genera. Oceana accounts for the other 50 to 70 genera.

One type of orchid is even a well-known food source, the genus *Vanilla*. *Vanilla planifolia* is native to Mexico. The seed pods from this plant are used to make vanilla flavoring. Some of the more common household orchid genera are:

- ❖ **Brassolaeliocattleya** – an orchid hybrid that includes parentage from three different genera: Brassavola, Cattleya and Laelia

- ❖ **Cattleya** - the corsage orchid

- ❖ **Cymbidium** – a waxier orchid, also used for corsages

- ❖ **Dendrobium** – the spray orchid, because it is found in flower arrangements

- ❖ **Doritaenopsis** – a smaller moth orchid

- ❖ **Miltoniopsis** – also known as Miltonia - the pansy orchid

- ❖ **Oncidium** – the dancing lady orchid

- ❖ **Paphiopedilum** – the lady's slipper orchid

- ❖ **Phalaenopsis** – the moth orchid

- ❖ **Vanda** – a showy, fragrant orchid

I include a table at the end of this book that summarizes some of the characteristics of each of these orchid species.

# Understanding How Orchids Grow

While orchids aren't difficult to raise, they are different from normal household plants. You can't fall back on how you take care of your African violet. In order to be successful at raising orchids, it's important to understand how orchids grow in the wild. You will notice I use the word "raising", not "keeping alive." It's much easier to keep an orchid alive - the difficulty comes in correctly meeting its needs to get it to flower again.

Orchids are considered perennial herbs, meaning that they lack any permanent woody structure. In tropical, or warmer, climates, orchids stay green all year and cycle through different growth phases. In temperate, or colder climates, native orchids will die back in the fall like any other perennial plant and grow again the following spring. There are three types of growth patterns in orchids:

❖ **Terrestrial orchids** naturally grow in soil or debris on the forest floor and use the soil for support. These types of orchids are most like other plants because they grow upright in soil.

❖ **Epiphytic orchids** naturally grow on another plant, such as a tree, although they are not parasites. These types of orchids have aerial roots which securely fasten the orchid to the tree's bark. Moss or debris usually gathers where the orchid attaches to the tree.

❖ **Lithophytic orchids** naturally grow on or near rocks. As with epiphytic orchids, aerial roots attach the orchid to the rock and moss or debris adds to the growing substrate.

These last two types of orchids can actually get all of the water and nutrients they need from the air, rain, and debris around them. This occurs because of three evolutionary adaptations:

❖ Orchids grow very slowly, so smaller amounts of nutrients are needed at one time.

❖ Orchids can absorb moisture and nutrients through their leaves as well as their roots.

❖ Orchid roots have a sponge-like material around them that absorbs and stores moisture for the root to take up as needed. The root is actually a thread-like strand inside the spongy structure that you see.

Many of the more common orchids that you may consider buying are epiphytic or lithophytic, meaning that they don't really need the pot and soil to survive. In their native environment, they would be hanging off a tree or attached to a rock somewhere. The pot is merely for our convenience. I've included the growth type in the Glossary at the end of this book.

As mentioned above, epiphytic and lithophytic orchids produce aerial roots which, as the name suggests, are roots that start growing from the stem into the air. An interesting fact about these types of orchids is that their roots do not naturally grow down. Most terrestrial plants have specialized cells at the end of their root tips that produce starch and make the tips heavier. Gravity has a greater effect on the tips pulling them down. The process is called gravitropism. That's why if you mistakenly plant a tulip bulb upside-down, the roots will come out of the top and turn to grow down. Epiphytic and lithophytic orchids don't have these cells and, therefore, don't particularly care which way their roots grow. Most of them are used to hanging out of trees.

Orchids are further categorized by *how* they grow. Monopodial orchids (meaning "one foot") grow upward on a single stem, producing leaves on alternating sides. The flower spikes on a monopodial orchid appear from bud nodes where the leaf attaches to the stem. Monopodial orchids can grow aerial roots anywhere along the stem. With my first few orchids, I felt compelled to somehow get these roots submerged in soil. I have since realized that aerial roots are perfectly happy growing right where they are. Phalaenopsis, Doritaenopsis, and Vanda orchids are monopodial.

Sympodial orchids have a stem, called a rhizome, which grows horizontally across the media. New growth appears from the end of the rhizome and grows upward. Each new growth shoot may have as few as one leaf. The flower spikes on sympodial orchids will come from the top or sides of this new shoot. Sympodial orchids often have a pseudobulb,

which is a thickened portion of the stem that functions as food and water storage.

Brassolaeliocattleya, Cattleya, Cymbidium, Dendrobium, Miltonia, Oncidium, and Paphio-pedilum are sympodial orchids.

There is no real advantage to one type of growth over the other; except that from my experience, monopodial orchids produce more flowers when they are in bloom. A single flower spike on one of my Phalaenopsis can have anywhere from six to eighteen flowers; and it often produces more than one spike. Phalaenopsis blooms can also last for three months. The exception to this would be my Cymbidium plant. This plant produces one or two bud spikes at a time which can have eight to ten flowers per spike; but it usually doesn't bloom as often as my Phalaenopsis or Doritaenopsis orchids.

Orchid Care: Finding the Right Light

First, a very brief botany lesson. Plants are autotrophs which means they make their own food. Orchids do this with a process called photosynthesis. The key ingredients of photosynthesis are light, water and carbon dioxide, with light being the prime ingredient. Without sufficient light, orchids can't make enough sugars to grow and bloom. However, with too much light, the orchid will dissipate the excess light as heat into their leaves which will scorch and dry the leaves. Also, the duration of light is as important as the intensity of light. You can't make up for shorter daylight hours by upping the intensity.

The first thing I did when I brought my new Phalaenopsis orchid home twelve years ago was go online and research what kind of light it needed, so I knew where to place it in my house. The article I read explained the foot-candles of light my orchid would need for each season. Seriously? How many people have light meters sitting around in their junk drawers? After many months of experimenting, I found that my little Phalaenopsis orchid was most happy in my north facing bay window. However, as it got bigger, I had to move it to a window that has brighter light.

If we go back to how orchids grow in the wild, it's fairly easy to figure out what they would like in your home. It's much easier to watch the color and texture of your orchid's leaves, than deal with a light meter. It's also not necessary to seasonally move your orchids or use supplemental lighting.

The exception to this is if you live in a far northern or southern latitude that does not provide 6 – 8 hours of sunlight a day at certain times of the year.

Phalaenopsis orchids are native to Southeast Asia, northern Australia, and areas in between. These areas have tropical and subtropical climates which means the climate is consistently wet, hot, and has a lot of light. In nature, Phalaenopsis orchids grow hanging off the lower part of a tree in the shade under the forest canopy. While they get a lot of sunlight, they are never hit with direct sunlight. In your home, mature Phalaenopsis orchids would like an east or west facing window. These locations provide bright, but not direct light. You can also set them on a table near a south facing window as long as the direct sun does not reach them.

Phalaenopsis and Doritaenopsis orchid leaves are usually larger and broader than other orchid species. The tops of these leaves should be a medium green color. The underside of the leaves can have a burgundy or red color, especially on new growth. The leaf should be firm and sturdy. If it is getting too much sun, its leaves will blanch, wrinkle or turn yellow. Dry patches may also appear where the leaf has been sunburnt. If the plant is getting too little light, the leaf will become a darker green, soft and floppy. If the plant is not getting enough light, new growth or bud spikes will not appear.

Another species that likes this type of lighting is Oncidium. These plants also like bright, filtered light. Oncidium leaves should be a bright green color. Dark green leaves mean they don't have enough light; and, reddish colored leaves mean they have too much light. Miltonia also likes diffused light, but will need brighter light to bloom, just not direct sunlight.

Cattleya and Brassolaeliocattleya orchids are two types of orchids that need more sunlight. Cattleyas are epiphytic and native to the tropical rain forest of South America. However, these orchids typically grow higher up in a tree, where they are only partially covered by the canopy. They like bright light. Cattleya leaves should be stiff; and they will have well developed, hard pseudobulbs if they are getting enough light. Cattleya and Brassolaeliocattleya orchid leaves should be a light, almost yellowish, green in color if they are getting the right amount of light. If their leaves turn a darker green, they need more light.

If their leaves turn all yellow or develop white patches, they  need shading during mid-day. Remember even though these orchids like bright light, they still grow under trees.

I live in southeastern Pennsylvania. At that latitude, I can keep my Cattleya and Brassolaeliocattleya orchids in a south facing window all day during the winter months. In the other months of the year, I use a sheer curtain at the window to filter the summer sun or back the pots away from the window out of the direct sunlight. If you live at a lower latitude, you may need to shade them during mid-day year round or try putting them in an east facing window.

Other orchid species that need higher light requirements are Cymbidium, Dendrobium, Paphiopedilum, and Vanda. Like the Cattleyas, the leaves of these orchids should be light green.

Yellow leaves means too much light and dark green leaves mean too little light. A red color to the leaves means that the orchid needs to be moved immediately because its leaves are being "burnt" by too much sun. A red color to the pseudobulb, but a normal leaf color, means the plant is at its limit of light intensity. If this happens, just back your orchid away from the window a little.

I live in a temperate climate. During the summer months, my orchids get an average of fourteen hours of sunlight, with the high of a little over fifteen hours occurring in June. During the winter months, they get an average of ten hours of sunlight, with the low of a little over nine hours occurring in December. I have never found the need to use artificial light. If you live at a latitude which gets fewer hours of sunlight per day than this, you may need to supplement with artificial light in the winter months. Remember that the duration of light is as important as the intensity of light. The best way to tell if your orchid is happy with the amount of light it is receiving is to make sure that its leaf color and texture is correct. You also have to watch the light hitting your plant as the seasons change. When the sun dips lower in the sky, it may come through a window more directly.

To summarize, watch the color and texture of your orchid's leaves to see if they are getting the right amount of light:

❖ If the leaves turn a darker green color, the plant needs more light. Plants use chlorophyll, which has a green color, in the photosynthesis process. If the plant is not getting enough light, it will produce more chlorophyll in an attempt to use more of the available light. The excess chlorophyll turns the leaves a darker color.

14

❖ If the leaves turn yellow, dry or develop white patches, the plant is getting too much light. The plant will dissipate excess light as heat into its leaves. This heat will dry and scorch the leaves.

❖ If the pseudobulbs become soft or shriveled, the plant may need more sunlight.

❖ If the pseudobulbs turn red but the leaves remain the correct color, the plant is at its limit of light. You may want to back the plant away from the window a little or move it to a window that gets less direct light.

❖ If the leaves turn red, the plant is being sunburnt and needs to be moved immediately to a less sunny location.

❖ If flower spikes do not develop or develop with very few flowers, the plant needs more sunlight.

❖ If you do need to move your plant to a stronger light source, do it gradually to give the plant a chance to adjust to the higher light levels.

❖ Move your orchid away from a high light source when it begins to flower, as the flowers can fade. This is the time to move it to a very prominent place in your home – remember, the reason you're raising the orchid is to enjoy the flowers!

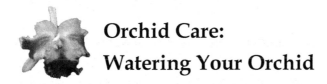

Orchid Care:
Watering Your Orchid

This is where most orchid collectors go wrong. They end up drowning their new orchid plants. More is not better when it comes to watering your orchid. As a general rule of thumb, if you're not sure if you should water your orchids, wait a day or two and then water it.

Keep in mind that most of the common household orchids are epiphytic, which means they are used to growing in the air. Their roots are exposed to the air and are watered by the consistent rainfall and humidity in the areas they live in. Epiphytic orchid roots never sit in a pool of water. Between these drenching rains, the roots have an opportunity to dry out.

Orchid roots do *not* like sitting in water. I cannot emphasize that enough – do not let water collect in the bottom of your orchid's pot. That's why orchid pots are supposed to have holes not only on the bottom, but also along the sides or up the center. While those pretty ceramic pots that many new orchids come in are lovely decorations, they are death knells for your orchid plant. If you water your orchid in the ceramic pot, the water collects in the bottom and rots the roots.

As mentioned earlier, orchid roots, leaves and pseudobulbs are designed to collect and hold water. Unlike other types of plants, orchid leaves absorb water and nutrients; and, orchid roots have a "sponge-like" coating around them called velamen, that can absorb moisture right from the air.

If you were to dissect an orchid root, you would find a thread

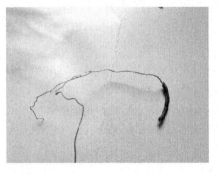 running through what looks like a sponge. That thread is the root. The rest of the material is capturing and holding water and nutrients for the root to absorb as it needs them.

Unless I have a very small orchid plant, I water my Phalaenopsis, Doritaenopsis, Oncidiums and Miltonia orchids every one to two weeks. Yes, I said "weeks". Smaller plants are watered once a week; and, older, larger plants are watered every 10 days to 2 weeks. As long as the leaves on these plants remain sturdy, and the pseudobulbs remain plump, the plant is getting enough water.

The leaves on distressed plants soften, wrinkle or curl. This can mean they are getting too much or too little water. You'll know which way to go with your watering depending upon

 how you have been watering the plant.

If the newer pseudobulbs begin to shrivel, the plant needs more water. I should note here that once a pseudobulb shrivels, it will never "unshrivel" or plump back out. This

doesn't mean that the orchid is still getting too little water. I should also note that, just like people, pseudobulbs will naturally wrinkle with age. So, watch the newer pseudobulbs to tell if your plant needs more water.

Watering Cattleya, Brassolaeliocattleya, Cymbidium, Dendrobium, Paphiopedilum, and Vanda orchids is a little different because they receive more direct sunlight. The number of hours of sunlight per day and the intensity of the sunlight will affect how often they need to be watered. I water these orchids once a week, unless it's during their active growth period in the summer months. Then, it may be more frequently, depending upon how hot my window area becomes. Again, watch for the health of the leaves and pseudobulbs to determine if more water is needed. Err to the side of less frequent waterings.

If you are still not sure if your orchid should be watered, there are some easy ways to check:

❖ Feel the orchid media for dampness. Sphagnum moss in some types of media is a good indicator. It gets stiff when it's dry. Also, dig into the media with your finger to feel for moisture.

❖ Clear orchid pots are wonderful because you can see the media through the sides of the pot. When the moisture droplets are gone inside the pot and the media has turned lighter in color, it's time to rewater.

❖ Check the weight of your orchid. After a while, you will recognize how much lighter your orchid feels when it is dry.

Watering an orchid is also done differently than for other house plants. I have been guilty of walking past my African violet, not being able to remember when I watered it last, dumping the half glass of water I was carrying into the pot and calling it a day. This is an example of how NOT to water an orchid.

Again, think about how the orchid grows in the wild. Most are hanging from trees, getting drenched every few hours. For the most part, nothing accumulates near their roots for any length of time. Even the debris that may get caught there is washed away and replaced on a regular basis.

The best way to water an orchid plant is to mimic this. Move your orchid pot to your sink and run water over the soil until it comes out of the bottom. Ideally, if you have a sprayer attachment, spray the leaves of the orchid as well as the media. Orchid leaves like to get wet since they would naturally grow in a humid environment. Let the pot sit there for 5 to 10 minutes and repeat the process. Orchid media is made of chunks of bark, lava rock, sponge rock, cork, granite, or sphagnum moss. By running water through the soil twice, it allows more moisture to be absorbed.

Doing this in the sink, allows the water to drain out before you put the plant back in its saucer. The best time to water your orchid is early in the day. This allows any water collected on the leaves to dry out before night.

Just as the best way to check if your orchid is getting enough light is to look at the color of its leaves, the best way to check if your orchid is getting the right amount of water is to observe its leaf, pseudobulb and root systems. If an orchid is getting too much water, it will generally rot from the bottom up. Orchid leaves should be firmly attached to the stems; newer pseudobulbs should be plump and firm; and the roots should be firm and white, yellow or green in color. Brown, black, or mushy roots have rotted and need to be removed. These are good indicators that your orchid is getting too much water.

One of my earlier mistakes of over-watering was with a Phalaenopsis orchid. The plant actually fell out of the pot because the roots had rotted off. Sometimes if a Phalaenopsis or Doritaenopsis orchid is getting too much water, its lowest leaves can turn yellow and begin to rot where the leaf attaches to the stem.

The type of water you use to water your orchids is only important if your water is very hard or softened chemically. Basically, your orchids will like the same type of water that you drink. Hard water will cause mineral accumulation in the orchid media. If your water is extremely hard, flush the orchid pots every few waterings with spring or distilled water to remove the excess minerals. If your water is chemically softened, it can leave salt accumulation around the roots, which can burn them. In this case, I would buy spring water for your orchids.

One last area to mention that is associated with watering is humidity. Since orchids naturally grow in humid tropical or sub-tropical forests, it's reasonable to assume that they need high humidity. In their natural environment, orchids have to get the water they need from the moisture in the air or from the rain that lands on them.

However, we are keeping our orchids all bundled up in soil. This helps to maintain water around their root systems. Most orchids will do just fine with humidity in the 40 – 70 percent range. It doesn't matter to the orchids if they get their water through their roots in the soil or through their roots and leaves in the air. I don't run around misting my orchids to keep up the humidity and they are perfectly happy. The exception to this rule is any orchid that is mounted on bark or grown without soil. Vanda orchids, for example, are usually grown in wooden, open-slat baskets without soil. In these cases, the roots are hanging in the air and regular misting is necessary.

Using a sprayer attachment when watering is an easy way to keep up humidity for your orchid. This is pretty much all the humidity they'll need unless your house is like the Sahara Desert. During the winter months when the air in my house may be drier, I just put the orchids back in their saucers before they're done draining. This allows some water to pool in the saucer which then evaporates and provides the orchids with more humidity. I buy saucers that have little ridges inside to set the pot on. This way I can keep the lower portion of it filled with water without soaking the roots in water.

This plan works well with all of my orchid species, except the Dendrobiums. Dendrobium orchids are a little bit fussier. Dendrobiums really like their light and humidity. The additional light causes the plant to dry out faster. The easiest way to handle this is to keep water in their saucers.

One final item to note is the presence of algae. If you have a clear pot, you may notice algae growing in the orchid media. With a clay pot, the algae may grow around the outside of the pot, especially the area sitting in the saucer. Algae is not a problem as long as you are watering your orchid as mentioned in this chapter and allowing the media to dry out between waterings. Algae can be an indicator, however, that too much water is staying in your orchid media between waterings. If you see an algae accumulation in or around your pot, you should cut back on your watering by a day or two. Also, as mentioned in the chapter, "Repotting Your Orchid," don't mistake algae for healthy, green roots. Unlike terrestrial plants, orchid roots have chloroplasts in them and can photosynthesize. Remember they are usually hanging in the air.

To summarize, when it comes to watering, less is better. Watch the texture of the leaves, the color of the roots, and the plumpness of the pseudobulbs:

❖ Most orchids will thrive with humidity in the 40 – 70 percent range. This means that unless your house is very dry, your orchids will do just fine without misting, which raises the humidity around the orchid for about 5 minutes.

❖ Watering with a sprayer attachment and allowing water to sit in the saucers (not near the roots) will increase the humidity around your orchids.

❖ Dendrobium orchids may need to be misted depending upon the amount of light and heat they are receiving. In this case, you will need to mist several times a day, focusing on the morning and early afternoon hours. You don't want to leave water sitting on the foliage overnight.

❖ Vanda orchids, and other bare root orchids, will definitely need to be misted several times a day as this is how the orchid will absorb water between regular waterings.

❖ Tap water is fine for watering orchids, unless your water is very hard or chemically softened. Frequent flushing with spring or distilled water can help. If your water is chemically softened, the use of spring water is preferred.

Orchid Care:
Feeding Your Orchid

The first thing to remember about orchids is that they grow very slowly; which means that they metabolize nutrients very slowly. This also means that they absorb nutrients slowly compared to your other plants. So, if you normally feed your house plants a full dose of fertilizer, once a month, you'll be wasting food on your orchids and causing a salt build up in the pot.

Epiphytic orchids get all of the nutrients they need from the debris that collects around their roots in the trees. Terrestrial orchids get their nutrients from the organic matter in the soil. In both cases, bacteria in this debris slowly breaks down the organic matter and provides the orchid with a steady, low-dose of nutrients.

There is an adage that goes with feeding orchids, "feed weakly weekly." Use a low-dose of fertilizer on a schedule of three weeks of feeding to one week off. For three weeks in a row, you should fertilize your orchid after each time you water it. That keeps a low dose of fertilizer available for the orchid at all times. Then the fourth week, thoroughly water your orchid to wash out any accumulated salts. Some orchid fertilizers are already set up to be dilute just for this reason and will recommend feeding once a week, so read the labels first. If the label says to feed once a month, the fertilizer dose will need to be cut to ¼ of what is recommended.

Most fertilizers are a combination of dry salts which need to be dissolved in the water. No matter how hard you try, you will still have some undissolved salt floating around in the container. I use an old, cleaned out gallon milk container to mix my fertilizer. It allows me to shake the solution to get it thoroughly mixed. I also prefer using liquid fertilizer because the salts are already dissolved for me.

The problem with salts is that they like water and will absorb it from their surroundings. So, if these salts accumulate near an orchid root, they can actually absorb the water from the root, causing the root to dehydrate or "burn". If this happens, you may see the tips of the orchid's leaves turn black or dried. If you have your orchid in a clay pot, another indicator of salt accumulation is white crystals on the outside of the pot. You can feel the crystals if you scrape your finger across the pot. When you see these crystals on your clay pot, it means they are present in the orchid soil, which can be harmful to the orchid. To correct this, I would thoroughly clean the outside of the clay pot and thoroughly flush the orchid media to remove the salt accumulation. If the crystallization continues on the outside of the pot, you may have to repot the orchid and change the media.

Picking a fertilizer is pretty simple. First, let me give you a brief primer on fertilizers. When you go out to buy a fertilizer, you will notice three numbers on the container (in the form X-X-X). These are the macronutrients in the fertilizer, or the nutrients with the highest concentrations. The first number is the percent, by weight, of nitrogen; the second is phosphorus; and the third is potassium. The orchid fertilizer I use is a 19-4-23, which is designed for well water.

Orchids use the nitrogen for their leaf and stem growth. Phosphorus is used for root and flower development and potassium helps with overall plant tissue health. There may be other macronutrients listed, such as calcium. There also may be micronutrients listed, such a magnesium, copper, sulfur and iron, which orchids need in trace amounts to aid in overall growth and flower development.

Finally, it is not necessary to buy "bloom booster" orchid food. Most orchids bloom just fine with regular orchid food. Remembering a feeding schedule for your orchids is one thing; remembering when to switch over to the bloom booster food is something else. This is supposed to be fun, not a chore. I've found using the regular orchid food works just fine and my orchids bloom consistently for me.

Also, make your feeding schedule easy. This is not rocket science and doesn't have to be exact. I "flush" my orchids the first watering of each month. This means I do not fertilize and I run the water through them for a longer period of time. This may not come out exactly to one flush for every three waterings, but it is close enough. Finally, as described in the *Orchid Growth* chapter, you should stop fertilizing for about one month during your orchid's rest phase.

To summarize, fertilizing orchids should not be a chore. It's mainly common sense when you understand how orchids grow in nature:

❖ Buy an "orchid" fertilizer, not just a generic plant fertilizer. Orchid fertilizers have the necessary secondary elements that the orchids need, such as the micronutrients listed above.

❖ Buy a "non-urea" orchid fertilizer. Fertilizers commonly use urea to provide the nitrogen. The problem is that urea takes a really long time to break down, so you're not getting as much nitrogen to the orchid as you think.

❖ Buy a liquid fertilizer. It makes mixing easier and eliminates the problem of undissolved salts.

❖ Remember to take at least one week off a month from fertilizing. This week is used to thoroughly flush the orchid media with water to remove any accumulated salts or minerals. If you have hard water, you may have to adjust this schedule to more frequent flushings.

❖ Blackened or dried leaf tips can mean there is an accumulation of salts or minerals that are affecting the root health. Immediate flushing or repotting is required.

❖ Fertilizing should only occur after the plant has been thoroughly watered. You don't want to fertilize dry media. You also shouldn't fertilize any plants that are showing signs of lack of water. Thoroughly water the plant and don't fertilize it until it recovers.

❖ Fertilize only in the plant's active growth or blooming phase. More fertilizer is not better. Excess fertilizer accumulates as salts and minerals around the roots.

Orchid Care: Finding the Right Temperature

This was another area of orchid care that was frustratingly complicated when I first started raising orchids. Orchid care books and websites that I looked at talked about ideal daytime temperature ranges, ideal nighttime temperature ranges, and ideal seasonal temperature ranges. I found myself placing small thermometers at the base of my orchid plants to check what the temperature was.

The reality is that orchids like the same temperature ranges as people. Most of the common orchid genera like a daytime temperature of 65 – 85 degrees F and a nighttime temperature of 55 – 70 degrees F. Remember that orchids are adaptable and somewhat flexible. So, keeping your house in the 70 to 75 degree F range is fine for most of the orchid species. An exception to this rule is the Cymbidium. Cymbidium orchids prefer cooler temperatures both during the day and at night.

You can also compensate for a lower daytime temperature by placing your orchids on a windowsill. Even filtered sunlight will provide some warmth, especially during the summer months, which is an orchid's growing period. This also allows for a lower nighttime temperature when the sun is gone.

All orchids do like cooler nighttime temperatures. During the day, the sunlight and warmth prompt the orchid to produce carbohydrates and use these carbohydrates to make new foliage. Even though the sunlight is gone at night, warmer temperatures keep the orchid making new foliage. This leads to beautifully large orchid plants with no flowers. When the temperature drops at night, the orchid is cued to store away its carbohydrates for future use, which is the making of flowers. If you can find your orchid a spot on or near a windowsill, the drop in temperature between day and night should be enough to keep it happy.

Most orchids are tolerant of temperatures as low as 55 degrees F. As a matter of fact, Phalaenopsis orchids are cued to put out bud spikes in the fall when temperatures drop to this level. Most orchids, however, will not tolerate temperatures much over 85 degrees F. Above this, they will begin to go into heat stress. You can check if your orchid is doing alright by checking its leaves.

To summarize:

❖ Most common orchid species like the same daytime temperatures as you do. Keeping them near a window can increase the daytime temperature if needed.

❖ If the orchid leaves or pseudobulbs become shriveled or soft, the plant may be heat or cold stressed. Place a thermometer in the location and measure exactly how high or low the temperature is going.

❖ Orchids need cooler nighttime temperatures, especially in fall when they will be setting flower spikes. This can be accomplished by placing the orchids on a windowsill where the temperature will drop at night. Sometimes, orchids need to be coaxed into producing bud spikes, especially Phalaenopsis orchids. You can do this by moving your orchids at night into a cooler area of your house, like a garage, for a week or two in the fall. The temperature can be as low as 55 degrees F.

Orchid Growth Cycles

Orchid plants cycle through three different phases. They have a rest phase which, as the name suggests, is when your orchid pretty much does nothing more than just sit there and look nice. No new growth or flower spikes will appear; although, it can have flowers on an old flower spike which have not dropped off yet. Then, the orchid will go into a growth phase which is when it will add new leaves in the case of monopodial orchids or grow new stems in the case of sympodial orchids. Finally, it will enter its blooming phase which is when flower spikes will appear.

Under normal conditions, orchids will cycle through these

three phases. I say "under normal conditions" because I have an older Phalaenopsis orchid that has been blooming constantly for the last two years. After about a year, I tried forcing it into a rest phase by cutting off its bud spikes (drastic times require drastic measures). New ones grew back. That's when I decided that it was perfectly happy living the way it was; and I let it go. It's still blooming; and it has managed to grow new leaves at the same time, although the new leaves are smaller than the old ones.

Any monopodial orchid will grow up by producing new leaves at the top. This picture shows the new, tiny leaf starting at the center of the old leaves on one of my Phalaenopsis

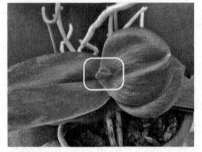 orchids. A monopodial orchid may only grow one new leaf during its growth period. However, its older leaves will also grow larger.

Sympodial orchids grow differently. They grow horizontally across the soil. A new shoot will appear from the old growth that just had the flower spike. Some sympodial orchids will only produce one new shoot during each growth phase. This picture is of one of my

Oncidium orchids. Note the new growth coming from the bottom of the old growth. Other sympodial orchids will produce two or more new shoots. Usually, each of these new shoots will produce a  bud spike during the next blooming phase in the cycle.

When your orchid has finished blooming, cut off the bud spike. Cut back watering it by a day or two; and stop fertilizing it for a month to let it rest. Then begin your normal watering/fertilizing schedule. You should see leaf growth or new shoots appear. Let your orchid put all its energy into growing until it's time for it to bloom again.

To summarize, orchids will normally cycle through three growth phases:

- ❖ **Rest Phase** – light watering, no fertilizer

- ❖ **Growth Phase** – normal watering and fertilizer

- ❖ **Blooming Phase** – normal watering and fertilizer

Getting Your Orchid to Bloom Again

Contrary to what most people think, orchids want to bloom. They are genetically programed to bloom in order to propagate the species. Orchids are also creatures of habit, and are usually cued into blooming from environmental factors such as light, nutrients or temperature. They will usually cycle through their three phases and end up blooming at roughly the same time each year. Your home and your care moderate the environmental cues and keep the cycles pretty consistent.

I buy most of my orchids at flower shows which occur in March of each year. This means that the orchids I buy are usually blooming in March. They continue to bloom in February and March of each year. After the flowers fall off, I let the orchid "rest" for about a month.

In the temperate climate that I live in, my orchids go into their active growth periods in the spring and summer. During this time, I give them more water and regular feedings. At the end of summer, with the shorter days and cooler nights, they begin to form bud spikes. Remember my orchids are on windowsills or near windows, so the temperature around them drops slightly at night with the outside temperature. This approach works well for most orchid species. Basically, if you keep them happy with their growing conditions, they will flower.

Some orchids can be stubborn, however. For example, Phalaenopsis orchids will not bloom unless they get cooler temperatures at night for a few weeks. So, if you have your brand new Phalaenopsis orchid sitting in the perfect place on a table in the middle of a room, it may grow quite large, but will not bloom again unless you move it to a location that cools down at night. My Phalaenopsis, that has not stopped blooming for the last two years, is sitting in a north facing bay window. During the night, the temperature at this window naturally drops by a few degrees, which tells it to bloom. You can also move your Phalaenopsis to a garage in the fall for up to a week at night to give it cooler temperatures.

Repotting Your Orchids

Orchids should be repotted with new potting media about once a year. This is not done because they have outgrown their pots. As I mentioned in earlier chapters, orchids grow very slowly, so don't wait for your orchid to outgrow its pot to repot it. Rather, repotting is done to refresh their media. Again, remember how these plants grow in the wild. Most are hanging from trees where any organic matter that accumulates near them is washed away and replaced on a regular basis. Orchids don't like stale media or a buildup of salts from their fertilizer. Old media can break down and lead to root rot because it reduces the amount of air getting to your orchid's roots.

The best time to repot orchids is when they have finished blooming and are in their rest phase. In most cases, you can use the same pot to repot it, especially with monopodial orchids. Slow growth means it takes these types of orchids a while to outgrow their pots.

If your orchid is healthy and has been growing, taking it out of its pot may not be as easy as it sounds. Even a small orchid can have roots that have grown out of the bottom of the pot or are attached to the pot. Remember that these roots were designed to attach to tree bark and hold the orchid in a tree. You have to accept the fact that you are going to tear off some of the roots when you repot your orchid. This isn't going to be a problem, however, with a root system that is healthy and developed. It is often easier to remove the pot if you soak the orchid with water first.

Repotting is also a time to do some "spring cleaning" with your orchid. Healthy orchid roots are firm to the touch and white, yellow or green in color. Another little known fact about orchids is that their roots can photosynthesize, which is why roots that are in the sunlight will turn green when watered. Those roots that do not see the sunlight are usually white or yellow. This makes sense if you go back to the fact that these roots would normally be aerial roots exposed to sunlight in the wild.

Dead or rotting roots are brown or black in color and shriveled or rotting. These roots as well as any dead leaves should be removed. Sympodial orchids may also have sections of old growth stems that have died and need to be removed.

Once your orchid is cleaned up and ready to be repotted, you want to use a good quality orchid potting media. The type of media you use will depend upon the type of orchid you are repotting. And, yes, there are major differences in the types of

 media.

For example, this is a bowl of Phalaenopsis potting media. Phalaenopsis orchids like a little more moisture around their roots, so this soil has a lot of sphagnum moss in it, along with cork, lava chips, sponge rock and pine bark. I will mention at this point, that any orchid potting media should be soaked in water prior to repotting your orchids. You don't want your new potting media to suck the moisture out of your orchid.

In contrast, this is a bowl of Cattleya potting media. Cattleyas  like their soil to be well drained, holding minimal moisture around their roots. This soil has no sphagnum moss and is comprised solely of small Styrofoam chips, lava rock, pine bark and bits of compressed clay.

The pot that you use to repot your orchid should be just slightly larger than the root ball. Orchids like to fit snuggly in their pots; and, remember that they grow slowly. It's best to pick a pot made specifically for an orchid. These pots have larger holes in the bottom and/or slits along the sides. Or, newer types of orchid pots have an indentation up into the bottom of the pot which allows air to circulate throughout the center of the root system.

Most of the orchid pots that you find are made of plastic which has the advantages of being light weight and inexpensive. Plastic also retains water well, and doesn't absorb toxic salts. Some people, however, prefer the aesthetic quality of clay pots. If you use a clay pot, be aware that they absorb water, so the orchid media will dry out sooner. Clay pots also absorb salts from the fertilizer and can release them back into the media. If you use a clay pot, you may want to cut back on the amount of fertilizer that you use and flush the media longer when watering. As mentioned in an earlier chapter, do not use glazed ceramic pots that have limited or no drainage holes. These pots will allow water to accumulate around the orchid roots and rot them.

The color of the pot does not matter, as long as it has good drainage. Newer orchid pots are being made clear, which has the advantage of making it easy to tell when your orchid needs to be watered because you can see the moisture in the soil through the sides of the pot. You can also see the heath of the root system.

The first step in repotting is to put some moist orchid media in the bottom of the pot. Then hold the orchid in the pot, allowing the roots to stretch out. It's important not to force the orchid's roots into a tight little ball. With one hand holding the orchid at the proper height in the pot, drop media down around the roots with the other hand. After you have about an inch or two of media in the bottom of the pot, push down with your fingers to compact the media around the orchid roots. Remember that orchids like to feel snug in their pots.

Continue this process until you have reached the top of the pot. If you've done this correctly, you should be able to pick up the orchid by its stem and it won't come out of the media. If it does pull out of the media, you need to push harder with your fingers to compact the media tightly around the roots. Accept the fact that you will break some of your orchid's roots when you repot it. As long as it's healthy, the orchid will be fine and new roots will grow back.

The only other thing to mention about repotting is where in the pot to place your orchid. Monopodial orchids, like Phalaenopsis, should be placed in the center of the pot because they are going to grow up. The surface of the media should be just below its first set of leaves. Don't worry if you have aerial roots sticking out above this point. Because these orchids grow up, they usually don't need bigger pots as often as some other types of orchids. The only time these orchids need a bigger pot is when the root ball has become too big to fit in its existing pot or the leaves have grown to the point that it becomes top heavy.

Sympodial orchids, on the other hand, grow horizontally across the soil. This means that they can outgrow their pots sooner. You'll know when this happens as the orchid can actually begin to grow entirely outside the pot. When repotting sympodial orchids, it is sometimes necessary to cut off older growth or separate the stems into smaller clumps. If you thin or separate the orchid, remember to cut off the older growth and keep the end that has the newest growth. In general, sympodial orchids will produce their new growth, and thus bud spikes, from the stem that bloomed last. Sometimes, older growth stems that have been cut off can be coaxed into producing new stems, but I wouldn't count on this.

One final thing to note is that if you thin a sympodial orchid, keep at least four stems with the new growth. Sympodial orchids use the carbohydrates and water stored in the pseudobulbs to make new growth and to bloom. You want to make sure that you've left the plant with enough food and water reserves.

Finally, when repotting a sympodial orchid, remember that it  is going to grow horizontally from the last stem that bloomed. When placing it in its new pot, you should off-center the orchid placing the oldest growth near the side of the pot. This provides the most room for new growth.

The last thing you need to do after repotting your orchid is to water it to settle the soil around the roots. Orchids are actually way more resilient than we give them credit for. As long as there are still some healthy roots and the main stem is not rotted, your orchid should thrive after its repotting experience.

One final topic is what to do if your orchid has a lot of aerial roots. As I mentioned earlier, these roots are designed to grow in the air. They will be fine right where they are. Some people, however, don't like the look of their orchid with aerial roots sticking out all around the plant. You can correct this when you repot the orchid. After you have taken your orchid out of its old pot, put the entire root system in a bowl of water, covering any aerial roots you want to move. After 5 or 10 minutes, the aerial roots will have softened to the point that you can bend them down into the pot. Gently bend the aerial roots down and cover them with soil as you repot the plant. I should mention, however, that you will probably be fighting a losing battle as the orchid will just grow new aerial roots.

Picking Your First Orchid Plant

For those of you who are reading this book *before* buying your first orchid, I can offer some suggestions. First, on average it takes about five years for an orchid plant to be old enough to bloom. This means that someone has been caring for this plant for five years before you buy it. The quality of that care, along with the parentage of the orchid, will determine how sturdy and healthy the plant is. Second, some genera of orchids, such as Phalaenopsis and Doritaenopsis hybrids, are more forgiving than others. If you pick one of these, it will make your first orchid experience happier and less stressful.

You have three options for buying your orchid:

❖ By far, the best option is to buy directly from a reputable orchid grower. There will be a great variety of orchid genera and colors. Growers generally hand raise their orchids; and you know they will be healthy, well cared for, and ready to bloom if not already blooming. When it comes to orchids, you definitely get what you pay for. With that being said, orchid growers are not as commonplace as flower shops. Unless you live in tropical or sub-tropical areas, you probably don't live anywhere near an orchid grower.

The closest one to me is about 90 miles away; although, as far as I'm concerned, it's well worth the trip. The great majority of my orchids come from Waldor Orchids in Linwood, New Jersey. This grower has been in business since 1925 and has top quality plants. You can stop at the greenhouses, go to their website, www.waldor.com, or see their magnificent displays at the Philadelphia Flower Show.

❖ Like almost everything else in life, you can buy your orchid off the Internet. This is convenient and offers you an endless range of orchid colors and types; however, I would only do this if you know the reputability of the orchid grower. I have done this with great success; but only with growers I already knew, such as Waldor Orchids. If you are considering this, I would call the grower first and explain that you are a novice orchid collector. They will be able to help you with your choice and you may get a feel for whether or not you want to deal with that grower.

❖ Finally, almost every grocery store, garden center and home improvement store now sells orchids. The advantage to this is that the orchids will be cheap. The disadvantage is that these orchids have been mass-produced, usually from clones. Not surprisingly, most of these orchids will be the easy to care for Phalaenopsis or Doritaenopsis hybrids.

Whether or not you are buying your first orchid, I would whole heartedly suggest that you attend a flower show, if there is one near where you live. My personal favorites are the Philadelphia International Flower Show, which occurs the first week in March, and the Longwood Gardens Orchid Extravaganza, which occurs from January through March of each year. Both of these events are in southeastern Pennsylvania.

44

The real advantage of attending a flower show is that you will be able to see an amazing assortment of orchids. Usually the plants are labeled, so it's kind of like window shopping. I use my phone to photograph the orchids that I like in the show displays, along with their names. Then, I just take my phone when I go to buy my new orchid plants. Another advantage of being at a flower show is that there are usually marketplaces at the shows where you can buy plants. Many of the growers who have sales booths in the marketplace have also entered the show, so you know that their plants will be a good quality. The employees at these sales booths will be very knowledgeable about orchids and will be able to help you with your selection.

As I mentioned above, I would suggest that you buy a Phalaenopsis or a Doritaenopsis Hybrid orchid for your first orchid plant. Phalaenopsis orchids, or moth orchids, are denoted by a "Phal" in front of their name. Doritaenopsis orchids are a cross between a Phalaenopsis orchid and a Doritis orchid and are denoted by a "Dtps" in front of their name. A Doritaenopsis orchid is basically a smaller version of a Phalaenopsis.

I would suggest sticking with Phalaenopsis or Doritaenopsis orchids until you feel comfortable raising these types. Make sure you can get them to not only grow, but also to rebloom before moving on to another genus. If you are feeling brave after this, I would suggest you try a Cattleya or Brassolaeliocattleya.

Moving Your Orchids Outdoors

Living in a temperate climate, my orchids have no choice but to live indoors during the colder months of the year. However, one of the most common questions I get asked from my friends is should they move their orchids outdoors in the summer months. In theory, anytime the temperatures outdoors are consistently above 55 degrees F and below 85 degrees F, conditions would be favorable for orchids.

There are pros and cons to rotating your orchids from indoor to outdoor plants on a seasonal basis:

Pros:

❖ Being outdoors gives your orchids an environment that is closer to its natural habitat. This means that, depending upon where you live, humidity levels and temperatures will be higher outdoors in the summer months than in an air conditioned house.

❖ The natural daily changes in temperature can encourage your orchid to go into its growth or bloom cycle.

Cons:

❖ You can't control the environmental conditions outdoors. If, for instance, you get a period of extremely hot, dry weather, you will have to water your orchids more frequently, or even move them into cooler locations.

❖ Severe weather, such as thunderstorms, heavy rain, or high wind, can damage the leaves or pseudobulbs on your orchids. In my area, we get a lot of our thunderstorms late in the day or overnight. This means that water would sit in the crowns of monopodial orchids, which could lead to crown rot.

❖ Your orchids would become fair game for any pest or fungus out there. I have occasionally moved some of my orchids outdoors; and, more than once, found an ant colony living in the pot at the end of the summer.

If your orchids are happily going through their growth/bloom cycles indoors, my suggestion would be to not mess with success and leave them right where they are. If you have an orchid that is not growing or blooming, then you may want to consider moving it outdoors for the summer just to give it a change. Some orchids can be fussy until they get a little older, so maybe yours is a young plant that needs climate conditions closer to its native home.

Obviously, if you live in a tropical or sub-tropical climate, your orchids will feel right at home outdoors. Should you decide to move your orchids outdoors for any reason, I have the following suggestions:

❖ Keep them in a sheltered, at least partially shaded location, such as under trees. Remember that none of these orchids grow naturally in direct sunlight.

❖ Anchor their pots well into the soil or a pot stand. You don't want them blowing over in a storm. I've seen some orchid holders that attach to tree trunks.

These are good choices as long as your pot is se-
cured in the holder.

❖ Realize that they are going to dry out faster outdoors
because of the higher temperatures. Plan on watering
them every 3 to 4 days if you don't get rain. Smaller
orchid pots may have to be watered more often.

❖ Treat them with a pesticide and fungicide as soon as
you move them outdoors. I would suggest buying
chemicals designed for orchids. Keep up with the
treatments throughout the time your orchids are outdoors.

❖ Leave them outdoors until the temperatures start to
drop in the fall. You don't want to move an orchid
from a hot, humid outdoor environment directly into
an air conditioned indoor environment. The plant
will experience cold shock. You need to ease them
back indoors. Wait until the daily highs outdoors are
closer to the temperature indoors, as long as the
nighttime temperatures don't drop below 55 degrees
F.

❖ Plan on repotting them when you bring them back
indoors. This will give you a chance to clean out the
dead leaves and replenish the orchid media.

❖ Keep plants that were outdoors separated from those
that stayed indoors until you are certain that the outdoor plants have no pests on them, including fungal,
bacterial or viral infections.

Orchid Pests

As with any other plant, there are insects, fungi, and viruses that would like to live in or eat your orchids. Luckily, unless you live in a tropical or sub-tropical climate, most of these pests are not native to where you live. This is probably the most pressing argument for keeping your orchids as indoor plants – you limit the amount of pests they come in contact with.

There are several things that will determine how susceptible your orchid plants will be to pests (which in this context includes fungi, viruses, bacteria or actual insects):

❖ First and foremost is the health of your plant. Healthy, mature orchid plants are far less likely to be affected by any pest infestation. Make sure you are meeting all of your orchid's basic needs, and pests should not have a huge effect on your orchid.

❖ Almost as important is the type of orchid you have. For example, I have always struggled with aphids on my Cymbidium orchid, but never had a similar problem with my Phalaenopsis, Cattleya, or other orchid genus.

❖ The parentage of your orchids can also create potential problems. The inexpensive, mass-marketed orchids are being bred for qualities like age at first bloom, length of bloom time, color of flowers or number of flowers. The hardiness of the plant is not necessarily one of the major considerations. This can lead to plants that are more susceptible to pests.

❖ Other plants in your house can pass on problems to your orchids. For example, gardenias are susceptible to aphids and fungal infections. It's best to try to keep your orchids separate from any other plants.

❖ Moving your orchids outdoors can bring them in contact with pests. Make sure you treat them with pesticides and fungicides regularly while they are outdoors and before they come back indoors.

❖ If you notice a pest on one of your orchids, separate that plant from the others until you resolve the problem.

To summarize, keep your orchids healthy and you should be fine. Check the plants when you water them. If you find pest problems, treat them with an orchid pesticide or fungicide. Insect pests are usually the easiest to diagnose because you can see them. For example, aphids are small green insects usually seen on the leaves and stems. See Table II at the end of this book to diagnose common orchid problems.

Ice Cube Orchids

I would be remiss if I didn't address the topic of "ice cube orchids". First, I would hope that if you have read my book up to this point, you would realize the words "ice cube" and "orchids" should not be found in the same sentence. With rare exceptions, orchids were never meant to be in the same vicinity as ice in nature.

Ice cube orchids are an amazingly successful marketing campaign, however, that reduces orchid care to placing one ice cube a day in the orchid pot. The orchids are usually mass-produced, cloned Phalaenopsis orchids, with very hearty parentage. Phalaenopsis orchids are naturally very forgiving, so this is a good choice. The idea behind ice cube orchids is to make caring for an orchid seem easy and more people will buy them. Who can't remember to put one or two ice cubes in the orchid pot a day?

Also, Phalaenopsis orchids can keep their blooms for up to three months or longer. Combine this with the low cost of ice cube orchids; and, the average person isn't hesitant to buy an orchid. For a minimal amount of money and work, an ice cube orchid will usually bloom for a quarter of the year.

There are, however, three major downsides to this method of caring for orchids. First, the melting ice will keep the orchid media constantly moist. In most cases, orchid roots do not like to stay wet. They like to dry out completely between waterings. The constant moisture will contribute to root system rot. Orchids also like to have their media flushed out on a regular basis. This does not occur with melting ice cubes.

Second, orchids should be fertilized regularly with a weak solution of orchid fertilizer. The ice cubes provide no fertilizer for the orchid. To compensate for this, some ice cube orchids come pre-fertilized with granular fertilizer. This type of fertilizer provides more fertilizer than the orchid can use and isn't flushed out of the pot leading to salt accumulation in the media.

Finally, the melting ice takes heat out of the orchid media and keeps the orchid at a cooler temperature than it needs. While the ice gives the orchid enough water to keep the blooms it came with, it does not provide the conditions necessary for the orchid to grow and rebloom.

In summary, the intent of the ice cube orchid is to be an easy-care, inexpensive plant that will retain its flowers for up to three months. If you intend on keeping the plant past this time, or trying to get it to rebloom, you will probably have to change your care methods to those presented in this book.

Table I: Orchid Characteristics

Genus	Abbreviation	Light Levels	Soil Moisture	Bloom Duration
Brassolaeliocattleya	Blc.	Medium to High	Well drained	6 - 8 weeks
Cattleya	C.	Medium to High	Well drained	1 – 3 weeks
Cymbidium	Cym.	Medium to High	Moist	4 – 6 weeks
Dendrobium	Den.	Medium to High	Well drained	8 – 10 weeks
Doritaenopsis	Dtps.	Low to Medium	Medium Drainage	8 – 12 weeks
Miltoniopsis	Mltnps.	Low to Medium	Medium Drainage	4 – 8 weeks
Oncidium	Onc.	Low to Medium	Well drained	6 – 8 weeks
Paphiopedilum	Paph.	Low to Medium	Medium Drainage	4 – 6 weeks
Phalaenopsis	Phal.	Low to Medium	Medium Drainage	8 – 12 weeks
Vanda	V.	Medium to High	Well drained	4 – 6 weeks

Notes:

- Low to Medium light – east or shaded west facing window; or a bright north facing window.

- Medium to High light – west or south facing window. In the summer months, a south facing window will need to be shaded.

- Medium Drained – these orchids like moisture to be kept around their roots longer. Their potting media usually has sphagnum moss in it. They can usually be watered less frequently, when the moss becomes dry.

- Moist – These orchids like their media to be slightly moist at all times.

- Well Drained – These orchids like to be watered more frequently, but have the water drain out of their media quickly.

Table II: Troubleshooting Guide

Part of Plant	Problem	Solution
Leaves	newer leaves are darker green and floppy	needs more light
Leaves	newer leaves turn yellow, brown or black and drop off	move to a warmer location
Leaves	newer leaves are wrinkled and limp	needs more water
Leaves	newer leaves are misshapen, folded, or wrinkled	The orchid is distressed by one of the following reasons: • needs more water • needs cooler temperature • has root rot
Leaves	all leaves are turning yellow or red	needs to be shaded more
Leaves	leaves have brown dead spots on them	• needs to be shaded more. The leaves have been sunburnt • the plant is reacting to cold shock. Move it to a warmer location.

Part of Plant	Problem	Solution
Leaves	leaves turn red or black and drop off pseudobulb	needs to be shaded more. The leaves have been sun-burnt
Leaves	• older leaves are wrinkled and limp • older, lower leaves are falling off the stem	• needs less water • needs to be re-potted. The media has broken down. • the root ball is rotted[1]
Leaves	leaf tips are brown or dead	too much fertilizer. Flush the pot well.
Leaves	irregular black or brown spot	• fungal infection. Use fungicide • if an Oncidium orchid, move to a warmer location
Leaves	underside of leaves are sticky or have a brown/black residue	• wash the leaves with warm, soapy water • fungal infection. Treat with a fungi-cide
Leaves	oldest leaves dry, turn brown and drop off	normal aging pro-cess
Pseudobulb	wrinkled[2]	needs more water
Pseudobulb	turning brown or black from the bot-tom up	needs less water. The root ball is rotting

Part of Plant	Problem	Solution
Pseudobulb	older pseudobulb shrivels, turns brown and drops off	normal aging process
Pseudobulb	develops black or brown spots along the stem	▪ pseudobulb was bruised during handling ▪ fungal infection. Treat with a fungicide
Center Stem	new growth turns brown or black and falls off	the root ball has rotted[1]
Roots	light brown, shriveled and dried	▪ normal aging process[3] ▪ needs more water
Roots	black or mushy	the roots have rotted. Change the orchid media, remove the rotted roots, and water less frequently.

Part of Plant	Problem	Solution
Roots	tips are brown or black and dried.	▪ the roots are burnt from salt accumulation. Flush the orchid well with water when watering. Repot and replace the media. ▪ this is mineral toxicity from too much or the wrong type of fertilizer. Cut back on fertilizer amounts or change type of fertilizer.
Roots	tips are green, purple or red	this is a normal color, as long as the root is firm.
Roots	tips are the same color as the root – no new growth	this is normal if your orchid is in its rest phase.
Roots	aerial roots are shriveling and turning brown	needs more water
Buds or blooms	orchid doesn't produce bud spikes	one or more of its basic needs are not being met[4]

Part of Plant	Problem	Solution
Buds or blooms	bud spikes appear but buds shrivel and fall off	• your orchid is a juvenile plant and is too young to bloom. Cut off the bud spike and let it grow. • your orchid needs more water or humidity. Check for other signs of drought conditions with the plant. • the temperature around your orchid is changing too fast. This can occur when a vent is blowing air on the plant. • your orchid has been cold shocked. Move it to a warmer location. • your plant is stressed[5]
Buds or blooms	flower edges are clear or brown	• this is cold shock. Move your plant to a warmer location.
Buds or blooms	brown spotting on the flowers	treat with a fungicide

Notes:

1. Sympodial orchids, such as Cattleyas, can sometimes recover from root ball rot. Remove all dead roots and pseudobulbs and repot in new orchid media. Monopodial orchids, such as Phalaenopsis, cannot recover from center stem rot.

2. Once wrinkled, a pseudobulb will not "unwrinkle." Do not continue to increase the plant's water expecting the pseudobulb to plump back out.

3. It is normal for some of the older roots to dry up and die. As long as no more than a third of the root ball is like this, the orchid it fine. If the greater majority of roots are like this, the orchid needs more water.

4. As mentioned in the chapter, "Getting Your Orchid to Bloom Again," orchids are genetically programmed to bloom. If your orchid is not blooming, one or more of its basic needs (temperature, light, water, fertilizer) are not being met. Go back and review these chapters.

5. Sometimes when orchids become stressed for any reason, they will put out a bud spike in an attempt to procreate before they die. You should diagnose what's wrong with the plant, cut off the bud spike and let the plant grow stronger.

Glossary

Aerial roots – Orchid roots that grow from anywhere along the stem into the air. These roots do not need to be anchored in soil.

Bloom booster fertilizer – These fertilizers usually have higher amounts of phosphorus in them. The problem is that most also have lower amounts of nitrogen and potassium. Bloom Booster fertilizers are not needed to get orchids to bloom as long as the orchid is healthy.

Blooming phase – After the growth phase, orchids will begin to put out new bud spikes. Normal watering and feeding should be continued.

Brassavola – A genus that has 21 species of orchids, all of which produce a single greenish or white flower. These are usually a very fragrant orchid at night, as the night moth is their pollinator.

Brassolaeliocattleya – A transgenic, epiphytic orchid hybrid that includes parentage from three different genera: Brassavola, Cattleya and Laelia.

Bud node – This is an area along the stem, bud spike or the rhizome where new growth, bud spikes or flowers will appear.

Bud spike – This is a long, thin stem that the orchid produces. Flowers will appear along the bud spike. This is also sometimes called a flower spike.

Cattleya – An epiphytic orchid best known as the corsage orchid.

Cymbidium – A terrestrial orchid that has waxier flowers. It is also used for corsages.

Dendrobium – An epiphytic or lithophytic orchid that is often found in flower arrangements.

Doritaenopsis – These are smaller moth orchids that are mostly epiphytic, although some species are lithophytic. I should mention here that the powers that be have decided to reclassify the Doritaenopsis orchid as a Phalaenopsis orchid. That means that the genus Doritaenopsis no longer exists. However, I have found that most growers I've bought from still use the Doritaenopsis classification.

Epiphytic orchids – These orchids grow on another plant. Their roots are normally in the air and attach to the plant for support. Debris that catches around the roots provides the nutrients the plant needs. Epiphytic orchids are not parasites.

Growth phase – After a rest phase, the orchid will begin to grow new leaves or stems. At this time, normal watering and feeding should be resumed. If the orchid does not enter a blooming phase after this, lighting and temperature need to be checked to make sure they are meeting the plant's requirements to bloom.

Hybrid orchid – An orchid that is a cross between two or more species and has been bred for specific traits, such as amount of flowers, hardiness, or color of flowers.

Ice Cube Orchid – These orchids are usually a mass-produced, cloned, Phalaenopsis orchid. The idea behind these orchids was to make orchid care easy.

Laelia – A genus with 25 species of orchids known for producing multiple, very beautiful flowers on one stem.

Lithophytic orchids – These orchids grow on or near rocks. Their roots are normally in the air and attach to the rock for support. Debris that catches around the roots provides the nutrients the plant needs.

Miltoniopsis – An epiphytic orchid known as the pansy orchid because of the shape of its flowers. This orchid is also known as a Miltonia orchid.

Monopodial orchids – These orchids grow on a single stem. As the plant grows, leaves appear on alternating sides of the stem. Bud spikes appear between the leaves from the single stem. Examples of monopodial orchids are Phalaenopsis, Doritaenopsis and Vanda.

Oncidium – Mostly epiphytic with a few lithophytic orchids. Many species in this genus have odd and uniquely shaped flowers. One of the species is known as the dancing lady orchid because its flowers look like a woman in a dress.

Orchid fertilizer – A good orchid fertilizer is a 19-4-23. The numbers represent the macronutrients in the fertilizer, or the nutrients with the highest concentrations. The first number is the percent, by weight, of nitrogen; the second is phosphorus; and the third is potassium.

Orchidaceae – The scientific classification for the family that contains the orchid plant. The complete classification is:

- Kingdom – Plantae
- Order – Asparagales
- Family – Orchidaceae
- Genera – 880 different genera
- Species – 30,000 identified

Paphiopedilum – These are mostly terrestrial orchids, although a few species are epiphytic and lithophytic. These orchids are known as the lady's slipper orchid.

Phalaenopsis – Most of these orchids are epiphytic, although a few species are lithophytic. This orchid is known as the moth orchid because it resembles a moth in flight.

Pseudobulb – The thickened portion of a sympodial orchid stem. Pseudobulbs store food and water for the orchid plant.

Rest phase – After an orchid has bloomed, it will enter a rest phase. During this time, feeding and watering can be cut back.

Rhizome – The stem on a sympodial orchid. It grows horizontally across the media.

Root ball – This is the area directly below the stems in the soil that roots grow out of. This area should not be soft or mushy. The roots coming from it should be firm and white or green.

Sympodial orchids – These orchids grow horizontally and have more than one stem. New stems appear from the rhizome. These stems can have as few as one leaf. Bud spikes will appear at the top or sides of the new stems. Examples of sympodial orchids are Brassolaeliocattleya, Cattleya, Cymbidium, Dendrobium, Miltoniopsis, Oncidium and Paphiopedilum.

Terrestrial orchids – These orchids grow naturally on the ground in soil or debris. Their roots are in the soil and use the soil for support. These orchids are most like normal house plants.

Urea – An ingredient in some orchid fertilizers that provides the nitrogen. The problem with urea is that it breaks down too slowly to provide enough nitrogen to the plant.

Vanda – Epiphytic orchids that are very showy and fragrant.

Velamen – The sponge-like coating around an orchid's roots. The velamen retains water and nutrients until the roots can absorb them.

Index

Acknowledgements

I would like to thank Walter Off and his staff at Waldor Orchids for raising the many beautiful orchids that I have purchased from them over the years. Most of my orchids and my daughter's orchids that have won ribbons at the Philadelphia Flower Show came from their greenhouses. I would also like to thank Walt for collaborating with me on the orchid classes I am teaching by providing the orchids that class participants receive. Finally, Walt is a wealth of orchid-related information. I'd like to thank him for sitting down with me and educating me on some of the finer points of timing orchids, and for loaning me his copy of the out-of-print classic, *All About Growing Orchids* (Ortho Books, 1988.)

About the Author

Barb Schmidt has a bachelor's degree in chemistry and biology and a teaching certificate in secondary education. She is a member of the Orchid Society, Longwood Gardens in Kennett Square, Pennsylvania, and the Pennsylvania Horticultural Society (PHS), where she teaches orchid classes. Her orchids have won a variety of awards, including first place ribbons at the Philadelphia International Flower Show.

CPSIA information can be obtained
at www.ICGtesting.com
Printed in the USA
LVOW01s1519140716

496336LV00022B/999/P